CHR

With every blessing

+ Anthony Ely.

ENFOLDED IN LOVE series
General Editor: Robert Llewelyn

LOVE ALONE (*Thérèse of Lisieux*)
Michael Hollings

THE DART OF LONGING LOVE
('*The Cloud of Unknowing*')
Robert Llewelyn

THE DESERT OF THE HEART (*The Desert Fathers*)
Benedicta Ward SLG

ENFOLDED IN LOVE (*Julian of Norwich*)
Robert Llewelyn

THE HEART AT REST (*St Augustine*)
Dame Maura Sée OSB

IN LOVE ENCLOSED (*Julian of Norwich*)
Robert Llewelyn

LAMPS OF FIRE (*St John of the Cross*)
Sister Elizabeth Ruth ODC

LANDSCAPES OF GLORY (*Thomas Traherne*)
A M Allchin

LIVING WATER (*St Teresa of Avila*)
Sister Mary ODC

THRESHOLD OF LIGHT (*The Celtic Tradition*)
A M Allchin and Esther de Waal

CHRIST WITHIN ME

✝

Daily Readings
from the Anglo-Saxon Tradition
'Be, Lord, a Lovely Aid'

Compiled
with introduction by

BENEDICTA WARD SLG

DARTON · LONGMAN + TODD

First published in 1999 by
Darton, Longman and Todd Ltd
1 Spencer Court
140–142 Wandsworth High Street
London SW18 4JJ

ISBN 0–232–52330–4

A catalogue record for this book is available from
the British Library

Designed by Sandie Boccacci
Set in 8¹/₄/12pt Utopia by Intype London Ltd
Printed and bound in Great Britain by
Page Bros, Norwich, Norfolk.

For Robert Llewelyn
enfolded in love

Contents

✛

Foreword   xi
1. Bringing the Gospel   1
2. Receiving the Gospel   2
3. Preaching the Gospel   3
4. Monasteries   4
5. Churches   5
6. The Eucharist   6
7. Daily Bread   7
8. Repentance   8
9. Penance   9
10. Singing   10
11. A Cowherd Poet   11
12. Poetry and Prayer   12
13. The Cross, the Tree of Life   13
14. Faithful unto Death   14
15. Easter Vigil   15
16. Easter Morning   16
17. Trinity   17
18. God the Father   18
19. Christ our Light   19
20. Christ Within Me   20
21. Come, Lord Jesus   21
22. The Holy Spirit   22
23. A Spirit-Filled Life   23
24. Solitude   24
25. A Hermit and the Demons   25
26. Death of a Hermit   26

[vii]

27. Death of an Author	27
28. An Angelic Welcome	28
29. English Friends Abroad	29
30. Friendship to Death	30
31. Loyalty to a Lord	31
32. A King at Prayer	32
33. A Prayer of King Alfred	33
34. Praying Queens	34
35. A Princess, a Necklace of Light	35
36. Mary, Mother of God	36
37. Jesus the Child	37
38. Children	38
39. Travellers and Exiles	39
40. Hermits and Birds	40
41. Horses and Saints	41
42. Whales and Deep Waters	42
43. Contemplation	43
44. Our Father	44
45. Our Father	45
46. Psalms and Life	46
47. The Psalms	47
48. Work and Prayer	48
49. Scripture	49
50. A Treasury of Books	50
51. Prayers for Authors	51
52. True Poverty	52
53. Morning Prayers	53
54. Prayers of Desire	54
55. Peace	55
56. A Rainbow	56

57. An Alleluia Victory   57

58. Heaven   58

59. A Celebration   59

60. A Prayer for the Compiler of this Book   60

Abbreviations   61

Acknowledgements   63

[ix]

Foreword

✠

The series of *Enfolded in Love* books was begun in order to offer extracts from mainline Christian writings of the past for use in the spirituality of the present. They convey a sense of being part of a great cloud of witnesses whose insight into and experience of the mystery of Christ is a living reality still.

In this volume, I have drawn specifically upon that part of the Christian tradition which is nearest to us, and most our own by belonging to our land and our people. I have selected material for prayer and meditation from Latin and Anglo-Saxon writings which have survived from the sixth, seventh and eighth centuries in England. Why should the basis of a distinctively English tradition of spirituality, that is, the relationship between God and man in personal experience, be sought among the Anglo-Saxon invaders of Britain in the sixth century? Certainly there were Christians in these islands before that, but the records of them are rare; the written sources on which we can depend begin in England in the sixth century and concern the new coming of Christianity to the English from the Mediterranean world, transmitted through missionaries from Rome and from Ireland. It is the mixture of these with the culture of groups of sophisticated Germanic peoples that produced a golden age of Christian life and thought in England.

One of the main ways in which this new Christian tradition was both formed and transmitted was by the writings of the Venerable Bede. Many of the following passages are from his works, and I have followed his method in their arrangement: That is, just as he taught 'by word and by example', I have selected words and placed them together with examples. Words are signs of a way to God but so are actions.

This English tradition has been constantly handed on with a sense of friendship, and many other volumes of the *Enfolded in Love* series reflect this continuity. For instance, English as a written language was invented in the time about which Bede wrote, and in the fourteenth century, where the initial books in this series were placed, its flowering formed the first English theology at the hands of the author of *The Cloud of Unknowing* and of Julian of Norwich. Moreover, there is a more direct link between the seventh and the fourteenth centuries in one of Julian's specific references to the man she described as 'a kynd neyghbur and of oure knowinge', John of Beverley, who was the bishop who had ordained Bede. The beauty of Irish and Welsh volumes in this series find their context and are best understood not in isolation but among these Anglo-Saxons. It is to underline this that I have included some Irish material, and taken my title from a hymn associated since the sixteenth century with Patrick of Ireland.

These extracts concern all kinds of people, not only the great ones in politics or learning or church affairs. There are here some scholars and bishops, some nuns and monks and solitaries, some princes and kings, queens and princesses; but also a cowherd, a poet, a soldier, a beggar, as well as birds and animals. There is a prevalent sense in these extracts of a familiar and eager love of Jesus, together with a serious awareness of the dangers of the world and of unredeemed human nature. It is possible through these passages to walk with these men and women as friends and see how their lives became filled with the life of Christ, in pain and desolation as well as in wonder, love and praise.

Benedicta Ward SLG

1. Bringing the Gospel

✠

Augustine and his companions came to King Aethelberht bearing as their standard a silver cross and the image of our Lord and Saviour painted on a panel. They chanted litanies and uttered prayers to the Lord for their own salvation and the salvation of those for whom and to whom they had come.... As they went towards the city of Canterbury, carrying the holy cross and the image of our great king and lord, Jesus Christ, they sang this litany in unison:

'We beseech thee, O Lord, in thy great mercy,
that thy wrath and anger may be turned away
from this city and from your holy house,
for we have sinned, alleluia.'

O dayspring, brightness of eternal light
and sun of righteousness,
come and give light to all
who dwell in darkness and the shadow of death.

2. Receiving the Gospel

✠

One of his men answered King Edwin, 'The fire is burning on the hearth in the middle of the hall and inside it is warm, though outside the winter storms of rain and snow are raging. A sparrow flies swiftly through the hall; it enters in at one door and swiftly flies out of the other. For the few moments when it is inside, the wintry storm cannot touch it, but after that brief moment of calm it flies from our sight into the wintry storm again. So the life of man appears only for a moment, and what follows or went before we know nothing about. If this new teaching brings us more certain information, it seems to me right that we should accept it.'

It is said that the fervent faith and longing for salvation of the Northumbrians was so great that for thirty-six days Paulinus did nothing else but instruct the crowds who flocked to him from every village in the saving word of Christ and baptised them in the river Glen which was close at hand.

3. Preaching the Gospel

✝

Cuthbert often went round the villages, sometimes on horseback but more often on foot, preaching the way of truth to those who had gone astray. . . . Such was his skill in teaching, such his power of driving lessons home, so gloriously did his face shine, like that of an angel, that no one dared keep back from him the closest secrets of their hearts. He made a point of seeking out the steep rugged places in the hills which other preachers dreaded to visit because of their poverty and squalor. He was so eager to preach that he would sometimes be away a whole week or fortnight, or even a month, living among the rough hill folk, preaching and calling them heavenward by his example.

Preachers sprinkle water on their way wherever they go when, as well as preaching by word of mouth, they show themselves to be examples of good living to those who see them. What they proclaim comes from an inner fountain of wisdom, from gazing upon the joy of the kingdom.

4. Monasteries

✝

Benedict Biscop sent agents to France to look for masons to build him a stone church in the Roman manner which he loved so much... and glaziers (craftsmen as yet unknown in Britain) to glaze the windows in the body of the church. He was untiring in his efforts to see that his monastery was well provided for: the ornaments and images he could not find in France he sought out in Rome.... He returned with a great mass of books of every sort. He brought back an abundant supply of relics of the blessed apostles and Christian martyrs which were to prove such a boon for many churches in the land and he also brought back many holy pictures of the saints to adorn the church... thus, all who entered the church, even those who could not read, were able, whichever way they looked, to contemplate the dear face of Christ and his saints, even if only in a picture, to put themselves more firmly in mind of the Lord's incarnation, and as they saw the decisive moment of the Last Judgement before their very eyes, be brought to examine their conscience with all due severity.

5. Churches

✠

We must not suppose that only the building in which we come together to pray and celebrate the mysteries is the Lord's temple, for we ourselves who come together in the Lord's name are more fully his temple. . . . Let us avoid winter's image lest the Lord on coming into our hearts find them numb from the lack of love's ardour.

Although the labours of this age are burdensome and prolonged, whatever ends in eternal blessedness should rather seem short-lived and trifling. . . . Let us busy ourselves in building an eternal mansion by the mutual help of charity so that when our Lord Jesus Christ comes he may find us all with cheerful hearts and tireless in doing all the good which he has commanded us to do, and then may he bring us to the reward of the perpetual vision of him which he has promised.

6. The Eucharist

✠

I, Bede, servant of Christ ... was ordained deacon at the age of nineteen and at the age of thirty priest, both times through the ministration of the reverend Bishop John (of Beverley) on the direction of abbot Ceolfrid.

Cuthbert was so full of penitence, so aflame with heavenly yearning, that when celebrating mass he could never finish the rite without shedding tears. But, as was indeed fitting, while he celebrated the mysteries of the Lord's passion, he would himself imitate the rite he was celebrating, that is to say, he would sacrifice himself to God in contrition of heart. Moreover, he would urge the people who stood by to lift up their hearts and give thanks to our Lord God, himself lifting up the heart rather than the voice, sighing rather than singing.

7. Daily Bread

✟

By daily bread we can understand the body and blood of Christ of which he said 'Unless you eat of this bread' (John 6:54). Let us pray that in receiving His body and His blood, by means of that which we see with our eyes, we may receive that which we do not see, that is, Almighty God, since 'whoso eateth my flesh and drinketh my blood remains in me and I in him'.

Whenever we enter the church and draw near to the heavenly mysteries we ought to approach with all humility both because of the reverence due to the presence of the angels and because of the reverence due to the sacred oblation; for as the angels are said to have stood by the body of the Lord when it lay in the tomb, so we must believe that they are present at the celebration of the mystery of his sacred body at the time of its consecration.

8. Repentance

✠

Almighty God, have mercy upon your suppliant for I am not as so many of your servants are, sublime through contempt of the world, glorious in the merits of their righteousness, angelic with the adornment of their chastity, nor am I even such as those who after public crimes by doing penance have become devoted to you. Indeed if by the aid of your grace I have done anything that is good, I do not know from what motive I have done it, nor with what severity it will be judged by You.

Cuthbert, in his zeal for righteousness, was eager to reprove sinners, yet he was kind-hearted and forbearing in pardoning the penitent so that sometimes when wrongdoers were confessing their sins to him, in his pity for their weakness he would be the first to burst into tears.

In your holy name make me whole, O Lord,
free me from foes through the power of your love.
My soul shall live and passionately praise you
and your decrees shall help me in my doings.
I have gone astray like a foolish sheep,
ah, seek your servant, Lord,
for I have never forgotten your glorious behests.

9. Penance

✠

There were some ravens that had long been used to live on the island, and one day when they were building their nest Cuthbert saw them tear with their beaks the little guest-house of the brothers . . . and carry off in their beaks the straw with which it was thatched, as material for their nest. He checked them with a slight motion of his right hand, and bade them stop injuring the brothers. When they ignored his command, he said, 'In the name of Jesus Christ, go away at once and do not dare to stay any more in a place you are damaging.' Scarcely had he finished these words than they flew dismally away. After three days, one of the pair returned and found the servant of Christ digging. With its feathers sadly ruffled and its head drooping to its feet, with humble cries it prayed for pardon, using such signs as it could, and the venerable father, understanding what it meant, gave it permission to return. And having got permission to come back, it soon went off to collect its mate. Without delay, they both returned, bringing a worthy gift, namely a portion of hog's lard. And this the man of God used afterwards to show to the brothers who visited him and offered to grease their shoes with it, declaring how carefully men should seek after obedience and humility seeing that even a proud bird made haste to atone for the wrong it had done to the man of God, with prayers, lamentations, and gifts.

10. Singing

✠

From this time also men began to learn throughout all the churches of the English the way of singing in church which they had hitherto known only in Kent. Excepting James ... the first singing master in the church of the Northumbrians was Aeddi surnamed Stephanus, who had been invited from Kent by the most reverend man Wilfrid, the first among the bishops of the English race who learnt to deliver the catholic way of living to the churches of the English.

When the reverend festivals of God's saints came round and when between two choirs in the church abbot Sigwine sang the verses of the psalms among the brothers, they rendered in song the sweet sounding music of the flowing antiphon. And the lector, a man very learned in books, poured forth song to the general delight, singing in a distinct voice. And when, as the day went on, they completed the singing of the mass, the brothers accompanied their spiritual father to the altar with harmonious song. Moreover no man could describe fittingly how earnestly he desired to celebrate sacred solemnities with his monks at festivals, how the clergy rejoiced within their bounds, shaking the church they filled it with loud singing.

11. A Cowherd Poet

✛

In the monastery of the abbess Hilda there was a certain brother, Caedmon, who had lived as a secular man until he was middle aged; he had never learned any songs. So sometimes at a feast when for the sake of providing entertainment they had decided to sing in turn, when Caedmon saw the harp coming towards him, he would get up in the middle of the feast and go home. One night when he did this, he left his place at the feast and went out to the cattle-byre. He stretched himself out and went to sleep, and he dreamt that someone stood by him and called him by his name: 'Caedmon,' he said, 'sing me something.' Caedmon said, 'I cannot sing that is why I left the feast and came here.' The speaker said, 'Nevertheless, you must sing to me.' Asked Caedmon, 'What must I sing?' 'Sing', he replied, 'about the beginning of all created things.' Thus Caedmon began to sing in English verses he had never heard in praise of God the Creator and when he awoke he remembered all he had sung while asleep and added more verses in the same manner, praising God in fitting style.

12. Poetry and Prayer

✝

Now we must praise
the keeper of the kingdom of heaven
the power of the one who ordains all things
and the intention of his mind
the work of the Father of glory.
For he, the Lord of Glory,
set the beginning of each wondrous thing,
and he, the holy maker,
first created the heavens
to be a roof for the children of men.
Then he, the protector of human kind,
the Lord everlasting,
the almighty Ruler,
made mortals for this middle earth, the world.

Facing the inevitable journey.
no one will be so wise
that he will not need to consider,
before he goes hence,
what shall be decided for his soul
whether good or evil
when his day of death has been determined.

13. The Cross, the Tree of Life

✠

Unclothed Himself God Almighty
when he would mount the Cross,
courageous in the sight of all men.
I bore the powerful King, the Lord of heaven;
I durst not bend.
Men mocked us both together.
I was bedewed with blood.
Christ was on the Cross.
Then I leaned down to the hands of men
and they took God Almighty.

Behold the wood of the Cross
Whereon was hung the world's salvation;
Oh, come let us worship.

14. Faithful unto Death

Boniface encouraged his followers saying, 'Brothers, be of good heart, fear not those who kill the body for they cannot slay the soul which continues and lives forever. Rejoice in the Lord, anchor your hope in God, for with no delay he will give you the reward of eternal bliss and bring you to dwell with the angels in his heaven. . . . Endure with steadfast mind the sudden onslaught of death, that you may be able evermore to reign with Christ.' As he was speaking the frenzied mob of pagans, whom he had come there to baptise, rushed suddenly on them, with swords and all kinds of weapons, staining their bodies with their precious blood.

The confession of the holy Name which is here maintained in the midst of enemies, there in their own home country makes the victors glorious.

15. Easter Vigil

✠

And since we are made glad by this yearly solemnisation of the mystery of our Lord's resurrection together with our own redemption, let us strive, dearly beloved, to take hold of these mysteries by the inner love of our hearts and always hold to them by living them out. Let us sometimes keep them, like clean animals chewing them over by murmuring them with our lips, sometimes by gathering them together in the inner chambers of our hearts. Above all let us take care so to live that we may deserve to behold with joy the outcome of our own resurrection also.... He himself will lead us all into the dwelling place of heavenly peace which he promised to us of old where he lives and reigns with the Father in the unity of the Holy Spirit God throughout all ages. Amen.

16. Easter Morning

✛

The risen Christ made known to all of them the height of glory that the humanity he had assumed for the sake of humankind had reached. 'All power in heaven and earth' he said, 'has been given to me.' He was not speaking here about the divinity co-eternal with the Father but about the humanity he had assumed.

In the daybreak she came, the grieving Mary,
and summoned the other woman with her.
Sorrowing, these two sought God's victorious Son
alone in that earthly vault where they knew
that the men of the Jews had hidden him.

In the dawning there came a throng of angels
the rapture of those hosts
surrounded the Saviour's tomb.
The earthly vault was open;
the Prince's corpse received the breath of life.
The ground shook and hell's inhabitants rejoiced;
the young man awoke dauntless from the earth;
the mighty Majesty arose, victorious and wise.

17. Trinity

✝

Almighty God, Lord and Ruler of all,
Trinity, Father in the Son,
Son in the Father, with the Holy Spirit,
forever in all things,
existing before all things,
Lord, blessed by all forever:
I commend my soul into your powerful hands
so that you may watch over it
by day and by night, every moment of every hour.

There is only one God who is the base and foundation
of all kinds of good, from him they all come and return
to him again. And he rules them. . . . Just as all the stars
are illuminated and brightened by the sun, some more,
some less bright. So too the moon which shines only as
brightly as the sun illuminates it; when the sun shines
directly upon the moon, then it becomes fully bright.

18. God the Father

☧

The vision of God the Father is reserved for us as the fulfilment of faith, our highest good, as Philip understood when he said, 'Lord, show us the Father and it sufficeth us' (John 14:8). For it must be thoroughly understood that we shall see and possess the reality of that which we believe while living in faith.

Almighty Father on high
who shaped and formed the shining world,
and established the expanse of the earth,
I confess and freely believe
that you are the eternal and only God.
You are the Lord of life,
the Author of angels,
earth's Ruler,
you made the depths of the ocean
and gave power to the plentiful great stars.

19. Christ our Light

✠

Wilfrid whose faith was so great by now that he might have been called the light of Britain, was locked up in a pitch black dungeon and securely guarded. His guards hearing him continually singing the psalms, looked into the cell and found the darkness of night turned into day.

O Christ, eternal light,
never deserting those who believe in you,
the true light that lights everyone
that comes into the world:
in the beginning you marked the birth
of your servant Wilfrid with fiery glory
when he came forth from his mother's womb,
so now as he prayed in the darkness of prison,
you sent an angel to visit him
and bring him light
as you did to the apostle Peter
imprisoned in chains by wicked Herod:
Glory and thanksgiving to you, O Lord.

20. Christ Within Me

✠

I bind unto myself today
The power of God to hold and lead
His eye to watch, His might to stay,
His ear to harken to my need.
The wisdom of my God to teach,
His hand to guide, His shield to ward,
The word of God to give me speech,
His heavenly host to be my guard.

Christ be with me, Christ within me,
Christ behind me, Christ before me.
Christ beside me, Christ to win me,
Christ to comfort and restore me.
Christ beneath me, Christ above me,
Christ in quiet, Christ in danger,
Christ in hearts of all that love me,
Christ in mouth of friend and stranger.

21. Come, Lord Jesus

✠

Come now, High King of the Heavens,
in your own person.
Bring life and salvation
to us weary slaves in torment,
overcome by weeping salt bitter tears.
You alone are the cure of our great sufferings.
Seek for us who are captives on earth
and when you return thither
do not abandon such a multitude
but as a king show mercy upon us
Saviour Christ, Prince of heaven,
and let not devils dominate us still.
Give us the eternal joy of your glory
so that we whom you once created with your hands
may worship you,
glorious king of the host of heaven.

Christ gives testimony to his church when he announces
that he will come and like the bride in the Song of Songs,
the church answers 'Amen; come, Lord Jesus'. And this
she cries aloud daily saying, 'Thy kingdom come.'

22. The Holy Spirit

✟

My brothers, the Holy Spirit not only gives perfect tranquillity in the future but also in the present when he kindles our minds with the fire of heavenly charity. Our only rest in this life is to be filled with the love of God. We who have been breathed upon by the Holy Spirit in baptism and have taken up the pleasant yoke of the Lord's love, learning after his example to be gentle and humble of heart, even now enjoy some mark of that future peace that passes understanding, when we shall be like him for we shall see him as he is.

> With elation I embrace the Holy Ghost
> equally eternal with both Father and Son
> by the confession of all not three gods thrice named
> but one God who has all three names
> in the mystery of his nature,
> true and victorious
> benefactor of mankind, magnificent, eternal Spirit.

23. A Spirit-Filled Life

✠

Those who have been breathed upon by the Holy Spirit and have taken up the most easy yoke of the Lord's love, and are learning by His example to become gentle and humble of heart, experience even now a taste of future tranquillity. . . . They always rejoice to call to mind the face of their creator and thirst, too, for the full sight of him saying with the apostle John, 'We know that when he shall appear we shall be like Him for we shall see him as he is.'

O Almighty God, open wide my heart and teach it by the grace of your Holy Spirit to ask for what is pleasing to you. Direct my thoughts and senses so to think and to act that by a worthy manner of life I may deserve to attain the eternal joys of the heavenly kingdom. Direct my actions according to your commands so that, ever striving to keep them in life, I may receive for my deeds the eternal reward.

24. Solitude

✠

Now after he had completed many years in that same monastery, Cuthbert joyfully entered into the remote solitude which he had long desired, sought, and prayed for, with the good will of the abbot and also of the brethren. For he rejoiced because, after a long and blameless active life, he was now held worthy to rise to the repose of divine contemplation.

> Delightful I think it to be in the bosom of an isle,
> on the peak of a rock,
> that I might often see there
> the calm of the sea.
> That I might see its heavy waves
> over the glittering ocean
> as they chant a melody to their Father
> on their eternal course.
> That I might bless the Lord
> who has power over all,
> heaven with its pure host of angels,
> earth, ebb, flood-tide.

25. A Hermit and the Demons

✟

When Guthlac was keeping vigil at the dead of night with unceasing prayer, he suddenly saw the whole tiny cell filled with horrible troops of foul spirits.... When dawn was breaking Guthlac had won the victory over his enemies and he stood giving thanks to Christ ... and when later he was occupied as usual with his morning praises to the Lord Jesus, he turned his eyes aside for a moment and saw two of the demons ... standing and weeping and when he asked them why they wept they said, 'We mourn that everywhere our strength has been broken by your prayer and we bewail our lack of power against your strength; for we dare not touch you or approach you again.'

> Let God arise and let his enemies be scattered
> let them also that hate him flee before him.
> But let the righteous be glad and rejoice before God
> let them also be merry and joyful.

26. Death of a Hermit

✣

I, Herefrith, went in about the ninth hour and found Cuthbert lying in a corner of his oratory opposite the altar; so I sat down by him. He did not say much because the weight of his affliction had lessened his power of speech. . . . He passed a quiet day in expectation of his future bliss until the evening; and he also continued quietly in prayer through a night of watching. But when the usual time arrived for night prayer, he received from me the sacraments of salvation and strengthened himself for his death, which he knew had now come, by the communion of the Lord's body and blood. Raising his eyes to heaven and stretching out his hands aloft, he sent forth his spirit in the very act of praising God, to the joys of the kingdom of heaven.

I thank you, O Jesu, for making blessed in heaven those who die in you on earth and how much more those who lay down their blessed lives in and for your faith.

27. Death of an Author

✠

Bede said, 'I have lived a long time and the righteous judge had provided for me well all my life. The time of my departure is at hand and my soul longs to see Christ the King in all his beauty.' This he said and other things to our great profit, and so spent his last day in gladness until the evening. Then the boy of whom I spoke, whose name was Wilberht, said once again, 'There is still one sentence, dear master, that we have not written down.' And he said, 'Write it.' After a little the boy said, 'There, now it is written,' and he replied, 'Good, it is finished, you have spoken truly. Hold my head in your hands for it is a great delight for me to sit over against my holy place in which I used to pray, that as I sit there I may call upon my Father.' And so upon the floor of his cell, singing, 'Glory be to the Father and to the Son and to the Holy Spirit' and the rest, he breathed his last.

Christ is the morning star who when the night of this world is past promises and reveals to his saints the light of life and of everlasting day.

28. An Angelic Welcome

✢

Hilda was attacked by a fever which tortured her with its burning heat and for six years the sickness afflicted her continually, yet during all this time she never ceased to give thanks to her maker and to instruct the flock committed to her charge, both in public and in private.... On the night of her death, the nun Begu seemed to see the roof of the house rolled back while a light which poured in from above filled the whole place. As she watched intently, she saw the soul of Hilda the handmaid of the Lord being borne to heaven in the midst of that light attended and guided by angels.

> Lord of the angels, have mercy upon me.
> Guide me, king of the archangels.

29. English Friends Abroad

✛

When Boniface went from England to preach the word of God in Germany . . . he sent messengers with letters to the abbess Tetta, asking her to send Leoba to accompany him on his journey and share his endeavour. She was called Leoba, because she was beloved, for that is what Leoba means. When she came the man of God received her with the deepest reverence, holding her in great affection . . .

When later he set out to go into Frisia, he commended her to his brothers, affirming his wish that after his death, when she died her bones should be placed next to his in his tomb, so that they who had served God during their lifetime with equal sincerity and zeal should await together the day of resurrection. After these words he gave Leoba his cowl and begged and pleaded with her not to leave their adopted land.

The happy house
Where friend from friend divides not,
And what he loves he hath forevermore;
Take me, beloved, in thy prayer with thee
Where shall be no estranging thee and me.

30. Friendship to Death

✢

Both Benedict and Sigfrid were worn out with their protracted illness; they knew they were near to death and would never be fit to rule the monastery again. Their weakness gave scope for the strength of Christ to be perfected in them, but physically they were so weak that one day, when they both wished to see each other and talk before they died, Sigfrid had to be carried on a stretcher to the room where Benedict lay on his pallet. Their attendants set them side by side with their heads resting on the same pillow, a sight to move you to tears. Though their faces were close together they had not enough strength to turn to kiss each other and had even in this to be helped by the brothers.

There'll come a time
when brother speaks with brother,
there'll come a time when joy will feast on joy;
there is a time for all things, now for parting,
O love that knows no end and no alloy.

31. Loyalty to a Lord

✠

Byrhrtwold grasped his shield and spoke,
he was an old companion,
he brandished his ash-spear
and most boldly urged on the warriors:
'Mind must be firmer, heart the more fierce,
courage the greater, as our strength diminishes.
Here lies our leader, hewn down,
an heroic man in the dust.
He who now longs to escape will lament forever.
I am old. I will not go from here,
but I mean to die by the side of my lord,
lie in the dust with the man I love so dearly.'

They laid Him down, limb-weary,
they stood at the corpse's head,
they beheld there the Lord of heaven
and there He rested for a while
worn-out after battle.
We still stood there weeping blood
long after the dirge of the warriors
had soared to heaven.

32. A King at Prayer

✠

Before battle, King Oswald seized a cross which had been hastily made and called out to the whole army, 'Let us all kneel together and pray to the almighty, living and true God, to defend us in his mercy from the proud and fierce enemy. For he knows that we are fighting in a just cause for the preservation of all our people.'

Very often, King Oswald would continue in prayer from matins to daybreak and because of his habit of frequent prayer and thanksgiving it was his custom to place his hands on his knees with the palms turned upwards. It is also a tradition that he died with a prayer on his lips. When he was beset by the weapons of his enemies and saw that he was about to perish, he prayed for the souls of his army, 'May God have mercy on their souls.'

Tell not your grief to a lesser man; tell it to your saddle-bow and ride forth singing.

33. A Prayer of King Alfred

✠

Lord God almighty, maker and ruler of all creatures,
I beseech you on behalf of your mighty mercy,
and through the sign of the holy cross,
and through Mary's maidenhood
and through Michael's obedience,
and through the love
and merits of all your saints,
that you guide me towards you
better than I have done myself
and direct me better than I am able,
according to your will and my soul's need.
Strengthen my mind in your will
and to my soul's need,
confirm me against the devil's temptations,
and keep far from me foul lust and all iniquity;
protect me from my enemies visible and invisible;
teach me to perform your will,
that I may inwardly love you before all things
with pure thought and clean body,
for you are my creator and my redeemer,
my sustenance, my consolation,
my trust and my hope.
Praise and glory be to you now and forever,
world without end. Amen.

34. Praying Queens

On the east side of Canterbury stands an old church built in honour of St Martin when the Romans were in Britain, where Bertha, a Christian princess from Gaul and wife of Aethelberht of Kent, used to pray. Here Augustine and his companions used to meet with her to sing psalms, pray, say mass, preach and baptise.

Aethelburgh, the daughter of Bertha, married the pagan king Edwin of Northumbria and Pope Boniface wrote to her.

> Let it be your constant prayer that God in his mercy will bless and enlighten the king, so that you who are united in earthly marriage may after this life remain united forever in the bond of faith. Melt the coldness of his heart by teaching him about the Holy Spirit so that the warmth of living faith may enkindle his understanding.

35. A Princess, a Necklace of Light

All who knew Hilda, the handmaid of Christ and abbess of Whitby, used to call her mother because of her outstanding devotion and grace. . . . Before she was born, when her father was living in exile under the British king, where he was poisoned, her mother had a dream that he was suddenly taken away and though she searched most earnestly for him, he could nowhere be found. But suddenly, in the midst of her search, she found a most precious necklace under her clothes and as she gazed closely at it it seemed to radiate such a blaze of light that it filled all Britain with its grace and splendour. This dream was truly fulfilled in her daughter Hilda, for her life was an example of the works of light, a blessing not only for herself but to many. Not only ordinary people but also kings and princes sometimes sought and received her counsel when they were in difficulties.

36. Mary, Mother of God

✠

Mary says 'My soul magnifies the Lord' and this is true of her more than any of the saints, for she rightly exults with joy in Jesus, that is, in her special Saviour, because she knew that the one whom she had known as the everlasting author of salvation was, in his temporal beginning, to be born of her flesh; in the one and same person he would most truly be both her son and her Lord.

> O splendour of the world,
> now show towards us that grace
> which the angel, God's messenger,
> brought to you;
> reveal to the folk that consolation,
> your own Son.
> Then may we all rejoice
> when we gaze upon the Child at your breast.
> Plead for us now with brave words . . .
> that He may lead us into the kingdom of His father
> where free from sorrow we may dwell in glory
> with the Lord of the heavenly hosts.

37. Jesus the Child

I sing of a maiden that is matchless;
King of all kings to her son she chose.
He came all so still where his mother was,
as dew in April that falleth on the grass.
Mother and Maiden, was never none but she;
well may such a lady God's mother be.

The Virgin was seen coming,
the young Christ at her breast,
angels bowing in submission before them,
and the King of the universe saying it was fitting.

Mary, mother of miracles,
help us, help us with thy strength,
bless the food, bless the board,
bless the ear and the corn and the victuals.

The Virgin most excellent of face,
Jesus more surpassing white than snow,
she like the moon rising over the hills,
he like the sun on the peak of the mountains.

38. Children

✝

Cuthbert loved games and pranks and as was natural at his age loved to play with other children. He was naturally agile and quick-witted and usually won the game. One day a child of no more than three years old began to rebuke him for his idleness and indulgence in games ... Cuthbert took this good naturedly, listened indeed with rapt attention and soothed the child's feelings with a friendly show of affection. He forsook his foolish games at once and went home. From then on he showed himself more mature and earnest as the Spirit, who had spoken to him through the mouth of an infant, spoke to him now in the depths of his heart.

When I, Bede, was seven years old I was, by the care of my kinsmen, placed in the care of the reverend Abbot Benedict and then of Ceolfrid, to be educated. From then on, I spent all my life in this monastery, applying myself entirely to the study of the Scriptures, and amidst the observance of the rule and the daily task of singing in the church, it has always been my delight to learn or to teach or to write.

39. Travellers and Exiles

✠

Jesus be thanked,
from Brittany to a foreign country, [Cornwall]
here have I come; I will go on shore.
'Lord Jesus, kind heart, guide me to a good place
that I may worship my dear Christ
and Mary the Virgin flower.
I have come to land and am weary with travelling.
Mary, mother and maid,
if you have house or mansion here,
guide me to it, for indeed I should greatly wish
to make an oratory beside Mary's house.'

As they were nearing home, the dog which had been with them on the way ran ahead, as if bringing the news, and wagging his tail (Tobit 30:1).

This dog, which was a traveller and a companion of an angel, is like a preacher of the gospel, running ahead to announce salvation. Preachers also keep watch over souls committed to them, just as it is natural for dogs to repay those who are kind to them and watch always for the master's safety. And as the dog showed its joy by wagging its tail which is at the end of its body, so every sincerely believing teacher, who is a messenger of the truth, rejoices that his work is accomplished when he leads his people home.

40. Hermits and Birds

✠

One Lenten season, when Kevin ... knelt with his hands outstretched and lifted up to heaven through the window of his hut, a blackbird settled on it, and busying herself as in her nest, laid in it an egg. And so moved was the saint that in all patience and gentleness he remained, neither closing nor withdrawing his hand, but until the young ones were hatched, he held it out unwearied shaping it for the purpose. And for a sign of perpetual remembrance of this thing, all images of St Kevin show a blackbird in his outstretched hand.

The excellence of the hermit Guthlac's charity abounded to all creatures so that even the birds of the untamed wilderness and the wandering fishes of the muddy marshes would come flying or swimming to his call as if to a shepherd and they were even accustomed to take from his hands such food as the nature of each demanded ... for if a man faithfully and wholeheartedly serves the Maker of all created things, it is no wonder that all creation ministers to his commands and wishes.

41. Horses and Saints

✝

King Oswine gave bishop Aidan an excellent horse so that he could ride if any urgent necessity compelled him. Soon afterwards, Aidan met a beggar who asked him for alms. He at once got down and gave the horse with all its royal trappings to the beggar for he was extremely compassionate, a friend of the poor and a real father of the wretched. The King was told of this and said to him, 'Have we not many less valuable horses or other things which would have been good enough to give to the poor without letting a beggar have the horse I had specially chosen for you?' Aidan replied, 'O King, what are you saying? Surely the son of a mare is not dearer to you than a son of God?'

As Columba sat by the roadside, a tired old man taking his rest, up ran a white horse, his faithful servant, and coming to the saint he leaned his head against his breast and began to mourn, and his tears ran down as a man's might into the lap of the saint. When Diarmid would have driven the sorrowing creature away, Columba prevented him saying, 'Let be, let be, suffer this lover of mine to shed on my breast the tears of his most bitter weeping. For his Creator has revealed to him that his master is to go from him.'

42. Whales and Deep Waters

✞

Brendan and his companions found the whale Jasconius in the usual place, climbed out of their boat onto his back and sang to the Lord the whole night and said their masses there next morning. After the last mass, the whale swam away and all the monks cried out, 'Hear us, O God of our salvation, thou that art the hope of the ends of the earth and of them that remain in the broad sea.'

Columba said: I delight to be here, where I may see the splendid flocks of birds over the full-watered ocean, that I might see its mighty whales, greatest of wonders; that I might see its ebb and flow and flood-tide.

My thought roams beyond the confines of my heart, my mind roams widely with the ocean tide over the whales home, over earth's expanses . . . the lone flier calls and urges the spirit irresistibly along the whale's path over the waters of oceans, because for me the pleasures of the Lord are more enkindling than this dead life, this ephemeral land.

43. Contemplation

✠

The contemplative life is when a man who is thoroughly taught through the long practise of holy living and who is instructed by the sweetness of daily prayer and often goaded by the remorsefulness of tears, has learnt to set himself free from all the affairs of the world and to direct his gaze towards the one true love and has begun in the heat of his desire to taste beforehand the joy of everlasting bliss which will be experienced in the life to come and sometimes even, as far as is right for mortal men, to gaze upon the divine in the rapture of his mind. This life of divine contemplation comes especially to those who after long trial of monastic discipline, have learnt to live apart from men, with minds so much the freer to meditate on heavenly matters since they are set apart from earthly disturbances.

Treading the paths of the gospel,
singing psalms every hour,
an end of talking and long stories,
constant bending of the knees.
My creator to visit me, my Lord, my King,
my spirit to seek Him
in the eternal kingdom where He is.

44. Our Father

✠

Father of mankind,
I pray you for healing,
holy Lord in the heavens.
May this your name be hallowed now,
fast fixed in our minds, redeeming Christ,
fast established in our hearts.
May your kingdom come to us mortals,
wielder of mighty powers,
righteous Judge,
and may your glorious faith
remain in our hearts
for the length of our lives.
May your will be fulfilled among us
in the habitation of the kingdom of earth,
as clear as it is in the glory of heaven,
made both dear and lovely
for ever and to eternity.
Give us now today, Lord of men,
high King of the heavens,
our bread, which you sent into the world
as salvation to the souls of mankind:
that is the pure Christ, the Lord God.

45. Our Father

✠

Guardian of men,
forgive us our guilt and sins,
and pardon our crimes, the body's wounds,
and our wicked deeds,
although we often offend against you,
the almighty God, in your mercies,
just as we pardon on earth the crimes
of those who often do wrong against us,
and do not think to accuse them
of their evil deeds,
in order to have eternal life.
Do not lead us to punishment,
to the grief of affliction, nor to the testing,
redeeming Christ,
lest we, devoid of grace,
become out of enmity estranged
from all your mercies.
And free us now from the evil of every fiend;
we in our hearts
shall eagerly speak of thanks and glory,
Prince of the angels,
true Lord of victories,
because you have mercifully set us free
from the bondage of hell's torments
by your mighty power.
Let this be.

46. Psalms and Life

✠

In the monastery over which Ceolfrid presided a pesti-
lence carried off all the brothers who could read or
preach or sing the antiphons and responds to the psalms
except the abbot and one little lad who had been reared
and taught by him. . . . Together they went through the
whole Psalter but without singing the antiphons. But after
a week, being unable to endure it any longer, Ceolfrid
resolved that with the help of the boy the order of the
psalms with their antiphons should be restored and
the psalms again sung.

As the angels live in heaven, so live men on earth who
rejoice in the praises of God through the pure heart of
psalmody. No mortal man can fully declare the strength
of the psalms. In them is confession of sins, the tears of
the penitent, sorrow of heart. Here is foretold all the ways
of our redemption, the wonderful delight of heaven's
mirth. Here you will find the incarnation, the resurrection
and the ascension of the Word of God.

47. The Psalms

✠

In the psalms if you look carefully
you will find an intimacy of prayer such as
you could never discover by yourself.
In the psalms you will find
an intimate confession of your sins
and a perfect supplication for divine mercy.
In the psalms you will find an intimate thanksgiving
for all that befalls you.
In the psalms you confess your weakness and misery
and thereby call down God's mercy upon you.
In the psalms you will find every virtue if you are
worthy of God's mercy in showing you their secrets.

Blessed is he whose unrighteousness is forgiven
and whose sin is covered.
I will acknowledge my sin unto thee
and mine unrighteousness have I not hid.
Thou art a place to hide me in
thou shalt preserve me from all trouble.

48. Work and Prayer

✠

Owine, head of the household of Queen Aethelthryth ... stripped himself so completely of his worldly possessions that he left all that he had and dressed only in a plain garment and carrying an axe and an adze in his hands, he came to the abbey of Lastingham. He did this to show that he was not entering the monastery for the sake of ease but to work hard. As he was less capable of the study of the scriptures he applied himself more earnestly to manual labour.... One day when he was occupied with some task out of doors he heard the sound of sweet and joyful singing descend from heaven to earth.... They were angel spirits coming to summon the abbot Chad to heavenly joys which he had always loved and longed for.

Better is a stupid and unlettered brother, who, working at the good things he knows, merits life in heaven rather than one who being distinguished for his learning in the scriptures or even holding the rank of a learned man, lacks the bread of love.

49. Scripture

✝

Whether you attend to the literal meaning or seek
for its inner truth, in the Gospel you will always
find light.

The light of the Gospel illuminates the dark sayings of
the Law and pours upon it the brightness of a new grace.

> I wish, O Son of the living God,
> ancient and eternal King,
> for a secret place in the wilderness
> to be my dwelling;
> a lovely church decked with linen,
> a dwelling for God of heaven;
> then, bright candles over the holy white scriptures.

I pray you good Jesus, as you have graciously granted me
sweet draughts of the Word which tells of you, so you
will of your goodness grant that I may come at length to
you the fount of all goodness and stand before your face
forever.

50. A Treasury of Books

✣

Abbot Ceolfrid enriched the monasteries over which he presided. . . . He splendidly enlarged the collection of books which either he himself or Benedict had brought from Rome so that among other things he caused three copies of the whole Bible to be transcribed, two of which he placed in his two monasteries in their churches in order that all who wished to read any chapter of either Testament might readily find what they wanted.

> Here, here your rest, sure rest for all your hurt,
> Eternal harbour for your quiet anchorage,
> Shelter and refuge of unhappy men
> That's always open. . . .
> One love, O thou that readest, that shall be
> Thine to eternity,
> That sent to thee this mighty gift of books
> That reading thou mayst recognise thy Maker,
> King, Maker of all things, Father, Redeemer,
> The Saviour Christ to whom be glory.

51. Prayers for Authors

✠

Lord Christ, great Son of God, all-good, all-wise,
Man's Life, Salvation, Maker, Mender, Friend,
Sole Word of God, thou kindly giver of gifts,
Now give the feeble poet thought and words,
Bedewing the dull heart from living streams,
That I may say of thee what thou hast given
No tongue can speak ought worth without thee.

Great Father of light,
from whom comes every good and perfect gift,
you gave me, the humblest of your servants,
the desire and means to see
the wondrous things of your law and also grace
worthily to bring out of the treasures
of the prophetic volumes things new and old
for the use of my fellow servants,
remember me, O my God, for good.

52. True Poverty

✠

We are all God's poor; let us therefore respond to the poor who ask anything of us, that God may respond to us when we ask him for what we need. Who are they who ask of us? Those who are poor and weak and mortal. Of whom do they ask? Of those who are poor and weak and mortal. Those who ask and those who are asked are the same except for possessions. How can you ask anything of God without blushing if you have refused to give to others what you can so easily grant?

> When you sit happy in your own fair house,
> Remember all poor men that are abroad,
> That Christ, who gave this roof, prepare for thee
> Eternal dwelling in the house of God.

53. Morning Prayers

✝

In the first hour of the day, that is, at the sun's rising, we should praise God and eagerly pray to him that he, out of the tenderness of his heart, may enlighten our minds with the illumination of the true Sun, that is, that he by his grace may so clear our inward thoughts that the devil may not through harmful darkness lead us astray from the right path nor impede more than we can bear with the snares of sin.

Christ, my Lord and Saviour,
Son of God,
I raise my hands in prayer to your name.
Christ, my Lord and Saviour,
by whom I have been brought
through the darkness of night
safely to the light of morning,
keep me this day, Lord,
in all the minutes and seconds of each hour,
leading me unharmed
by your grace to glory.
So may it be.

54. Prayers of Desire

✛

Glory always to God
and the Lord our Saviour
both now and forever
and when amidst the pressures of adversity
we still live in the body
and are struggling apart from him,
and particularly then,
when the long-desired of all nations shall come
and deign to enlighten us
by the vision of his presence.
Meanwhile we deserve to sigh for him
and earnestly sing,
because one day in your sight
is better than a thousand.

Be, Lord, a lovely aid;
look upon me, O Lord,
and be swift to help me
in my most earnest need.

55. Peace

✠

There was so great a peace in Britain, wherever the rule of King Edwin reached, that . . . a woman with a new-born child could walk throughout the island from sea to sea and take no harm.

> God, the truest peace, we ask you
> to keep our hearts and minds
> in calm and in peace,
> for where there is peace
> you also are present
> and where you are, everything is yours.
> Come, then, O Lord, and so possess us
> that we may become a sanctuary
> for your Holy Spirit.
> Glory to you, Father,
> with your only begotten Son,
> by whom you give life
> with the Holy Spirit
> forever. Amen.

56. A Rainbow

✠

When the feast celebrating the anniversary of the death of Bishop Wilfrid was over, the whole company went out of doors to sing compline in the twilight. Suddenly a wonderful white arc shone before them in the sky; apart from lack of colour it looked exactly like a rainbow. We worshipped and praised the Lord for this sign, the Lord who is wonderful in his saints, for we clearly saw that he was with us, building a wall of protection around his chosen vineyard.

A rainbow was set about the throne (Rev. 4:3). The rainbow, which is caused by the rays of the sun shining upon the clouds, and was first set there after the Flood for a sign of mercy, so it shows us now how we are protected by varied colours of the saints who are filled with the light of Christ.

57. An Alleluia Victory

✠

During the season of Lent when the army was expecting a battle, the bishops Lupus and Germanus were in the camp, instructing the army daily and vast numbers were baptised. Still soaked in the waters of baptism the army set out when the Easter solemnities had been celebrated and bishop Germanus offered himself as their leader. He himself bore the standard and he instructed his men to repeat his call in one great shout. As the enemy approached, the bishop shouted 'alleluia' three times. A universal shout of alleluia followed and echoes from the surrounding hills multiplied and increased the sound. The enemy were smitten with dread fearing the very frame of heaven was falling upon them and fled. So the bishops won a victory without shedding blood by faith and not by might.

It is our custom to chant 'alleluia' more frequently and happily during the fifty days from Easter to Pentecost, remembering during this our earthly exile, this song of our homeland in heaven.

58. Heaven

☩

There was a very broad and pleasant plain, full of the fragrance of growing flowers. . . . So great was the light that flooded that place that it seemed to be brighter than the brightness of daylight or the rays of the noonday sun. In this meadow there were countless people in white robes, and many sitting around in great happiness.

By heaven we understand the Lord Jesus Christ, by earth, the church. We know that as a man is to a woman, so is heaven to earth. From heaven the church receives all its fruitfulness, 'every good and perfect gift cometh from above' (James 1:17). Just as your will is done in heaven which is Christ so may it be done in the church which is his body. As it is done in the heaven of just men, so may it be done also in the earth of sinners by their repentance.

> May your will be fulfilled among us
> in the habitation of the kingdom of earth
> as clear as it is in the glory of heaven,
> made both dear and lovely for ever and to eternity.

59. A Celebration

✠

I should like to have a great ale-feast
for the King of Kings;
I should like the heavenly host
to be drinking for all eternity.
I should like to have the men of heaven
in my own dwelling.
I should like to have
the vessels of charity to dispense.
I should like to have
the pitchers of mercy for that company.
I should like hospitality to be here for their sake;
I should like Jesus to be here always.

We are being nourished on food roasted on the gridiron
when we understand literally, openly and without any
covering, the things in the Scriptures that are said or
done for the health of the soul; we eat food from a frying
pan when by frequently turning it over we see what alle-
gorically corresponds to the mysteries of Christ; and
afterwards we search the oven for bread of the Word to
lay hold of the mystical riches of the Scriptures.

60. A Prayer for the Compiler of this Book

✠

And now that at length so great and hazardous a labour has been complete I beg and pray that if anyone shall think this little work of mine worth reading or copying out, they will also remember to commend to the Lord the author of the work for I have not laboured for myself alone but also for them. May I in return be rewarded by the vows and prayers of those who have benefited by my toil and may they by their good offices cause me to gain the right to and fruition of the tree of life, the odour and good report of which I have in some measure communicated to them.

Abbreviations

✜

Quotations have been taken from the following books. In some cases the translations are my own. I have also taken the liberty of emending some of the texts to fit the purpose of this book.

Bede (673–735)

EHEP   *Ecclesiastical History of the English People*, ed. and trans. B. Colgrave and R. A. B. Mynors, Oxford 1969

Homilies   *Homilies of the Venerable Bede*, trans. L. Martin and D. Hurst, 2 vols., Kalamazoo 1991

On Revelation   PL 93, cols. 129–207

On Habaccuk   *Commentary on the Canticle of Habaccuk*, trans S. Connolly, Dublin 1997

Alcuin of York (735–804)

Alcuin (a) *More Latin Lyrics*, trans. H. Waddell, London 1976

Alcuin (b) *De Psalmorum Usu Liber*, PL 101

ASMG   *Anglo-Saxon Missionaries in Germany*, ed. C. H. Talbot, London 1954

VC   *Life of St Ceolfrid*, trans. D. S. Boutflower, London 1912

VG   *Life of St Guthlac*, trans. B. Colgrave, Cambridge 1956

ASP   *Anglo-Saxon Poetry*, trans. S. A. J. Bradley, London 1962

CM   *A Celtic Miscellany*, trans. K. Hurlston Jackson, Harmondsworth 1951

**Texts from *The Age of Bede* ed. D. H. Farmer,
Harmondsworth 1951**

VSC	*Life of St Cuthbert*
VSW	*Life of St Wilfrid*
VA	*Lives of the Abbots*
VSB	*Voyage of St Brendan*

Acknowledgements

✠

1 EHEP 1,xxv
  Antiphon for the Magnificat during Advent

2 EHEP 2,xiii

3 VSC cap.9
  Homilies: 'Homily in Holy Week' 2,4

4 VA cap.5

5 Homilies: 'On the Dedication of a Church', 2,24

6 EHEP 5,xxiv
  VSC cap.16

7 Alcuin (b) col. 215
  Homilies: 'Homily in Advent', 1,4

8 Bede, *Commentary on St Luke*, PL 92, col. 553B
  VSC cap.ix
  Benedictine Office, ASP p.541

9 VSC cap.20

10 EHEP 4,ii
   Aethelwulf, *De Abbatibus*, ed. A. Campbell, Oxford
   1967, II, 495–506

11 EHEP 4,xxiv

12 'Caedmon's Hymn', ASP pp.3–4
   'Bede's Death-Song', ASP p.5

13 The Ruthwell Cross Inscription, ASP p.5
   Good Friday, Liturgy of the Veneration of the Cross

14 ASMG p.56
   On Revelation: 22,iv

15 Homilies: 'On the Easter Vigil', 11,7

16 Homilies: 'On Easter Morning', 11,8
   'The Descent into Hell', ASP p.392

17 *Book of Nunnaminster*, ed. Walter de Grey, London

1889, p.58
EHEP 5,xxi

18 On Revelation: 22,iv
From the Old English Benedictine Office, ASP pp.541–2

19 VSW cap.36

20 *St Patrick's Breastplate*, trans. C. Alexander, *Hymns Ancient and Modern*, London 1924, no.655

21 'Christ 1: the Advent Lyrics', ASP p.209
On Revelation: xxii,20

22 Homilies: 'On Pentecost', 11,17
'The Lord's Prayer', ASP pp.541–2

23 Homilies: 'On Pentecost', 11,17
Bede, *Commentary on Ezra and Nehemiah*, ed. D. Hurst, CCSL, CX1XA, Turnholt 1969, p.392

24 VSC cap.17
'St Columba's Island Hermitage', CM 222

25 VSC cap.34
Psalm 67

26 VSC cap.39
On Revelation: 14,xiii

27 'Cuthbert's Letter on the Death of Bede' EHEP
On Revelation: 2,xxviii

28 EHEP 4,xxiii
Book of Nunnaminster, pp.58–60

29 'Life of St Leoba', ASMG p.214
Alcuin (a) col.197

30 VA cap.13
Alcuin (a) col.185

31 'The Battle of Maldon', ASP p.527
'The Dream of the Rood', ASP pp.161–2

32 EHEP 3,ii

33 King Alfred's translation of Boethius in *Age of Alfred*, ed. S. Keynes and M. Lapidge, Harmondsworth 1983, p.137

34 EHEP 1,xxvi
   EHEP 2,xi

35 EHEP 4,xxiii

36 Homilies: 'In Advent', 1,4
   'Christ 1: the Advent Lyrics IV', ASP p.212

37 *Oxford Book of Carols*, Oxford 1964, no. 183, pp.390–1
   'A Prayer to the Virgin', CM 243

38 VSC cap.1
   EHEP 5,xxiv

39 'St Meriasek Arrives in Cornwall', CM 241
   Bede 'Commentary On Tobit' trans. T. Foley, in *A Bede Miscellany*, Liverpool 1999, 11, ix, p.57

40 Gerald of Wales, *A Journey Through Ireland* 11,28, trans. Helen Waddell, *Beasts and Saints*, London 1995, p.121
   VSG cap.38

41 EHEP 3,xiv
   Adamnan, *Life of St Columba*, trans. R. Sharpe, Harmondsworth 1991, 3,xxiii

42 VSB cap.27
   'St Columba's Island Hermitage', CM 222
   'The Seafarer', ASP p.329

43 Homilies: 'On the Feast of St John the Evangelist', 1,9
   'The Hermit', CM 224

44 'Our Father', ASP pp.539–41

45 Ibid.

46 VC cap.14
   Alcuin, Letter IV, 391, PL101, col. 497–8

47 Alcuin (b) col. 465
   From Bede's Abbreviated Psalter, in B. Ward *Bede and the Psalms*, Jarrow 1991, appendix

48 EHEP 4,iii

   Bede, *On Proverbs*, ed. D. Hurst, ccsʟ, CX1XA, Turnholt 1983,
   12:9, p.71

49 On Revelation: 4,viii

   'A Wish of Manchan of Liath', CM 223

   EHEP 5,xxiv

50 VC cap.20

   Alcuin (b) col.191

51 'On the Saints of the Church of York', in *Alcuin of York*,
   Stephen Allott, William Sessions, York 1974

   Bede, *Commentary on Ezra and Nehemiah*, ibid., p.392

52 Homilies: 'For Christmas', 1,vii

   Alcuin (a) p.179

53 Benedictine Office, ASP p.539

   Book of Nunnaminster, p.76

54 Bede, *Commentary on the 7 Catholic Epistles*, trans. D. Hurst,
   Kalamazoo 1965, p.156

   Benedictine Office, ASP p.539

55 EHEP 2,xvi

   Book of Nunnaminster, p.80

56 VSW cap.69

   On Revelation: 4,iii

57 EHEP 1,xx

   Homilies: 'Homily in Advent', 1,20

58 EHEP 5,xii

   Homilies: 'On the Easter Vigil', 11,6

   'Our Father', ASP p.540

59 'I should like to have a great ale-feast', CM 227

   Bede, *Commentary on 1 Samuel*, 11,85, p.87

60 On Revelation: Conclusion

✠

Thanks are due to the following publishers for permission to quote copyright material: Cambridge University Press for *The Life of St Guthlac* translated by G. Colgrave; Cistercian Publications Inc. for *Bede the Venerable: Homilies on Gospels* (Cistercian Studies Series: Numbers 110–111) translated by L. Martin and D. Hurst and *Bede the Venerable: Commentary on the Seven Catholic Epistles* (Cistercian Studies Series: Number 82) translated by D. Hurst; J. M. Dent (Everyman's Library) for *Anglo-Saxon Poetry* translated by S. A. J. Bradley; Four Courts Press for *Commentary on the Canticle of Habaccuk* translated by S. Connolly; Liverpool University Press for *Bede: A Biblical Miscellany* translated by W. Trent Foley and Arthur Holder; Oxford University Press for *Bede's Ecclesiastical History of the English People* edited and translated by B. Colgrave and R. A. B. Mynors, and Aethelwulf, *De Abbatibus*, II, 495–506, edited by A. Campbell; Penguin Books Ltd for *Texts from the Age of Bede* edited by D. H. Farmer, translation © J. F. Webb; *Alfred the Great* translated by S. Keynes and M. Lapidge and *The Life of St Columba* translated by R. Sharpe; Routledge for *A Celtic Miscellany* edited by K. Hurlston Jackson; St Paul's Church, Jarrow for *Bede and the Psalms* by B. Ward; Sessions of York for Alcuin 'On the Saints of the Church of York' in *Alcuin of York* by Stephen Allott; Sheed & Ward for *Anglo-Saxon Missionaries in Germany* edited by C. H. Talbot; Stanbrook Abbey for *More Latin Lyrics* by Helen Waddell, edited by Felicitas Corrigan.